Rev Up Your Writing in Letters and E-mails

BY LISA M. BOLT SIMONS • ILLUSTRATED BY MERNIE GALLAGHER-COLE

The Child's World®

Published by The Child's World®
1980 Lookout Drive • Mankato, MN 56003-1705
800-599-READ • www.childsworld.com

ACKNOWLEDGMENTS
The Child's World®: Mary Berendes, Publishing Director
Red Line Editorial: Editorial direction and production
The Design Lab: Design

PHOTOGRAPHS ©: Shutterstock Images, 6; iStockphoto, 12; Marco Piunti/iStockphoto, 18

ISBN 9781634070645
LCCN 2014959943

Printed in the United States of America
Mankato, MN
July, 2015
PA02261

ABOUT THE AUTHOR

Lisa M. Bolt Simons is a writer and teacher. She has published ten books with more on the way. Her writing has been recognized with awards and grants, including one to travel to Africa. Originally from Colorado, she lives in Minnesota with her husband and twins. Her Web site is www.lisamboltsimons.com.

ABOUT THE ILLUSTRATOR

Mernie Gallagher-Cole is a children's book illustrator living in West Chester, Pennsylvania. She loves drawing every day. Her illustrations can also be found on greeting cards, puzzles, e-books, and educational apps.

Table of Contents

CHAPTER ONE

An Introduction to Writing Letters and E-mails

Around 500 BC, a Persian queen wrote the first known letter. Since then, communication has gone through many changes. Jump ahead to the early 1970s. Engineers created a way to send messages on computers. These messages became known as electronic mail. Later, people shortened it to e-mail.

Writing letters using a pen and paper used to be common. It was the only way to communicate with those far away. But most people do not write letters like this anymore. Most people communicate by e-mail or other electronic messages. Sometimes a typed letter is attached to an e-mail. It is important to know the **form** and **content** of both letters and e-mails. Letters and e-mails may differ in some ways.

Through the ages, people have written on leaves, bark, papyrus, cotton, and linen. Metal, wood, bone, and goose quills were the pens. One kind of ink came from a fish.

Being able to write letters and e-mails is a valuable skill. Both forms of communication are good ways to stay in touch with family and friends. Plus, many workers write e-mails every day at their jobs.

Letters and e-mails communicate ideas and information to a reader. This information must be written clearly. Explanations are important. Facts, quotes, and examples help support the idea or information. Focus on one idea per message.

Suppose you are writing to a principal. Your letter or e-mail needs to have **formal** language. Now suppose you are writing to a friend or family member. Your letter or e-mail can have **informal** language. Either way, use language that is exact and appropriate to your audience.

10 Side Street

Anytown, MN 55555

October 17, 2015

Principal Murray

Roosevelt Elementary

1234 Avenue Way

Anytown, MN 55555

QUESTIONS
Who is the audience of this letter? How does that affect the language being used?

Dear Principal Murray:

   We, the students at Roosevelt Elementary, want to request more playground equipment. The equipment we have now is old. Some of it is missing.

   Students are outside for 15 minutes a day, five days a week. This adds up to over an hour a week. Several classes go out at one time and share the equipment. But some of the balls and nets are missing. The Hula-Hoops are mostly bent. We know equipment is not cheap. But we need new equipment. We are getting bored outside. We need to keep our bodies moving.

   We would like to make two suggestions. One, we would like to shovel snow this winter for donations. Two, we would like to have a carwash in the spring. We hope we can raise some money for new equipment.

Thank you for considering our request. We need new playground equipment, and we hope to help pay for it.

Sincerely,

David Shaffer

David Shaffer

Class President of Roosevelt Elementary

CHAPTER TWO

Form

A letter has a specific form. It includes two addresses, the date, and the **salutation**. It also includes the body, the closing, and the signature.

The first address is yours. On the next line, write the date. After that, put the address of the person you are writing to. Include the person's name and title.

The salutation is a greeting. It often starts with *Dear* followed by the person's name. In formal letters, use the person's title and last name, such as *Dr. Jones*. This is followed by a **colon**. If you know the person well, you may use an informal salutation. In that case, write the first name and a comma.

The body of the letter usually has three parts. The first part is the introduction. You state the main information or idea. The next paragraph gives details or examples. These sentences support the letter's main idea.

Many people put a signature at the bottom of their sent e-mails. This is not a signed signature. Instead, it is their typed name, title, and contact information.

Additional paragraphs can give more details. The last paragraph restates why the letter is being written. You can make suggestions or ask for something.

In formal letters, the closing is usually *Sincerely*. In an informal letter, *From* or *Love* is most common. Below the closing, write your name. If you are writing your letter by hand, you can just write your name. If you are typing your letter, leave four blank lines and type your name. Then write your signature in the blank space.

An e-mail is a bit different from a letter. An e-mail does not need the addresses or the date. In fact, the date is included automatically. But the salutation, the body, and the closing are the same. Of course, you cannot sign e-mails with a pen. So you will have to type your name.

The biggest difference between letters and e-mails is time. Letters can take days to arrive, but e-mails arrive within seconds.

4321 Booker Drive

Townville, CO 55555

August 13, 2015

Mayor Zak Salah

Townville City Hall

5678 Central Avenue

Townville, CO 55555

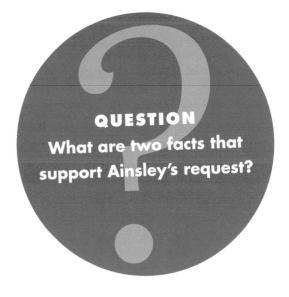

QUESTION
What are two facts that support Ainsley's request?

Dear Mayor Salah:

I am writing to ask for bike racks in Main Square Park. My friends and I ride our bikes there a lot. Our parents are worried our bikes will get stolen if we do not lock them. I think more children will play at the park if there are bike racks.

My mom just read a magazine article about children staying in shape. She said only 30 percent of children in the United States get moving every day. I think that number would go up in Townville if we had bike racks at the park. Main Square Park has lots of playground equipment. Children love going there. But not many children ride their bikes. Riding bikes to the park would be an added activity for children.

Please give us bike racks, Mayor Salah. It will encourage more children to be active. That will help people be healthier.

Sincerely,

Ainsley Jones
Ainsley Jones

CHAPTER THREE

Content

Your letter or e-mail may be formal or informal. But either way, you need to clearly explain your information or ideas. If your message is formal, you should be careful with your word choices. For example, the formal letter in Chapter 2 uses the word *children*. Using the word *kids* would be informal.

It is also important to use details. These details can be facts, definitions, or examples. They can also be **sensory details**. These include sight, sound, touch, taste, and smell. Quotes are also a good way to support your ideas or information.

Make sure your letter or e-mail is appropriate. Even if you are frustrated, choose words that will get your point across. You should not try to start an argument.

If your letter or e-mail is making a **request**, stick with one request. If you have more than one, your message may be distracting. Also, make sure your message reaches

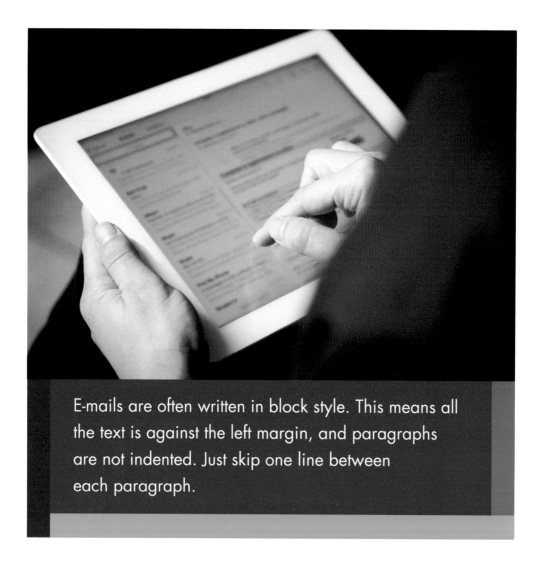

E-mails are often written in block style. This means all the text is against the left margin, and paragraphs are not indented. Just skip one line between each paragraph.

the right audience. For example, suppose your older sister wants to request a later curfew at the mall. Sending a letter or e-mail to a store will not target the right audience. Her letter or e-mail should go to mall security.

When moving on to a new idea, use words that connect your sentences. For example, *another* and *also* are helpful words when writing facts. *First*, *then*, and *next* help with **sequence**. Cause and effect words include *because* and *as a result of*.

Letters may seem like a thing of the past. E-mail is an important part of everyday life. But knowing how to do both will help you be a better writer, student, and worker.

Dear Grandma and Grandpa,

How are you doing? How has the weather been? Are you golfing a lot? Or is Grandpa hitting balls in the water? Ha-ha!

I wanted to tell you about our camping trip. It was so much fun! I took my friends Mason and Alex. Mom and Dad came, of course. And we brought the two dogs.

On our first day, we canoed to our campsite. There was a big hill, so we played Capture the Flag about a gazillion times. It was super fun!

On our second day, we fished by a small waterfall. Boy, did we catch a lot of fish! Dad cooked them up that night. We ate them with mashed potatoes. Yum!

On the third day, we just swam and played in the canoe. Mason kept adding water to the canoe so that it sank. What a joker! We couldn't stop laughing! That night, Dad told us scary stories. I wasn't very scared, but we slept with a flashlight on. Ha-ha!

We headed back home just as it started to rain. It was an awesome time!

See you at Thanksgiving!

Love,

Richie

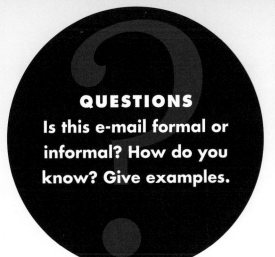

QUESTIONS
Is this e-mail formal or informal? How do you know? Give examples.

TIPS FOR YOUNG WRITERS

1. Check your writing to see if it makes sense. Read it aloud or read it to another person.

2. Do not use letters and e-mails only to complain. Write them to give compliments, too.

3. Ask your parents or guardians if they have a letter they wrote that you can read. Is it formal or informal?

4. Do not put an e-mail address in the *To* field until you are ready to send your message. This way, you will not accidentally send an e-mail before you have finished writing and editing it.

5. Make sure to put your return address in the top left corner and a stamp in the top right corner on an envelope.

6. Write a letter to the President of the United States. First, write it formally. Second, write it informally. How were the two letters different?

7. Read a novel that is written as a series of letters. Compare it to other novels that are not written this way.

8. Write a letter to a friend. Now write the same letter as an e-mail. Which do you prefer?

GLOSSARY

colon *(KOH-luhn):* A colon is a punctuation mark with one period on top of another (:). A colon can be used after a formal salutation or to introduce a list.

content *(KAHN-tent):* Content is what is written. The content of a business letter must be formal.

form *(FORM):* Form is how the parts of something are arranged or structured. The form of a business letter includes the date, salutation, and closing.

formal *(FOR-muhl):* Formal means fancy, showy, or elegant. The queen wore a formal dress to the banquet.

informal *(in-FOR-muhl):* Informal means ordinary or casual. The girl spoke to her best friend in an informal way.

request *(ri-KWEST):* A request is something you ask for. The boy made a request to stay outside longer, but his mother said no.

salutation *(SAL-yu-TAY-shun):* A salutation is a word or phrase that starts a letter. Most often, *Dear* is the word used in a salutation.

sensory details *(SEN-suh-ree DEE-taylz):* Sensory details are specific examples of the five senses. If you are describing a hot day, one sensory detail might be the feeling of sweat dripping down your face.

sequence *(SEE-kwens):* Sequence means order. A recipe's instructions are an example of a sequence.

title *(TYE-tuhl):* A title is a word that shows a person's job or status. *Dr.* and *Mrs.* are titles.

TO LEARN MORE

BOOKS

Minden, Cecilia, and Kate Roth. *How to Write an E-mail*. North Mankato, MN: Cherry Lake Publishing, 2011.

Minden, Cecilia, and Kate Roth. *How to Write a Thank-You Letter*. North Mankato, MN: Cherry Lake Publishing, 2012.

Proudfit, Benjamin. *Writing Letters*. New York: Gareth Stevens Library, 2014.

Warren, Celia. *How to Write Letters and E-mails*. Laguna Hills, CA: QEB Publishing, 2007.

ON THE WEB

Visit our Web site for lots of links about letters and e-mails:
www.childsworld.com/links

Note to Parents, Teachers, and Librarians: We routinely check our Web links to make sure they're safe, active sites—so encourage your readers to check them out!

INDEX